Bruised to Beautiful

Life Lessons from Bananas

By Annie Meehan

Bruised to Beautiful, Life Lessons from Bananas, © Copyright 2022 by Annie Meehan.

ISBN 979-8-9860054-1-6

Dedication

To all the coaches, counselors, and encouragers in the world that believe in bruised bananas and help to show them their worth on the journey to finding their own sweetness.

Praise for
Life Lessons from Bananas

Short, "Sweet", and Profound

I love how Annie shares her life experiences to show that, even though we might feel "bruised," we can still make something very sweet despite our previous experiences. I love her analogy using Banana Bread ingredients to live. Annie gives everyone hope that even though we may be bruised, we always have the choice to change the bruising and bitterness and make something sweet.

I know this is short, but hopefully it will help serve your purpose. I loved this story! Thank you for allowing me to read and review it. I hope that it will touch many people! More hope is needed in our world today!

Meriden Toombs
Author, *Natara*

Just like her *Pineapple Principle* book, *Bruised to Beautiful, Life Lessons from Bananas* is simple to follow, rich with impact, and creates a can-do attitude. Always inventive, Annie's new recipe provides the ingredients and steps for transforming your life. As an HR professional, mental health has risen to the top of the list for employee engagement and well-being. *Bruised to Beautiful, Life Lessons from Bananas* should be given to all employees as a guide toward mental health wealth. Combined with *The Pineapple Principle*, it could make for a powerful workshop in the workplace, especially when hosted by Annie herself.

Amy J. Allen, MSOHRD PHR
HR Professional

Annie Meehan can take an everyday piece of fruit, like a banana, and turn it into a thought-provoking analogy that becomes the foundation for an inspirational book. Annie's book will add the sweet ingredient you need in your life.

MJ Callaway CSP, CVP
Creator of
The Bounce-Up™ Principle

Bruised to Beautiful

Life Lessons from Bananas

Growing Into a Successful Adult

Why bananas? Why not lemons to lemonade? You see, my whole life I have heard, "Wow! You sure took the lemons you received growing up and turned them into lemonade."

But I know I needed a lot more than sugar, and water, and lemons to turn my dysfunctional childhood into a successful adulthood.

Have you ever felt like a bruised banana? I felt like a beaten and bruised banana most of my childhood.

My early years were filled with being beaten down by hopelessness, instability, insecurity, sadness, yelling, and a lack of the basics in life.

When we feel like a bruised banana, we have two choices-- though, as a child, it might feel like we have *no choices*.

It took me a long time to figure out what I needed to do to become who I was meant to be.

A bruised banana might get thrown away--or be the base for sweet banana bread.

I believe bananas have amazing lessons to teach us if we are willing to use them even when they are bruised and appear to be worthless.

Just like people.

When we feel beaten down by life we still have choices. Will we become bitter *or better*?

A bruised banana can just be thrown away.

Sometimes, I felt like throwing away my life.

But there is another choice.

A bruised banana can be used to add flavor and sweetness to make banana bread.

However, it takes more than a few ingredients to turn a bruised banana into a beautiful loaf of freshly baked banana bread.

My Wake-up Call

When I was 19, I had my first unplanned pregnancy. It was a wake-up call in my life.

As soon as I found out I was pregnant, I knew I needed to make some major changes. I wanted to be the kind of parent I never had, and that required me to make many changes and take a good long, hard look at my life, and focus on what was not working.

The baby's father was someone who I thought I loved and who said he loved me; however, he did not want to be responsible for a child.

I think he panicked and said, ina a rather negative tone, "Are you going to have an abortion or should we get married?"

I never dreamed of being proposed to that way and I said I was going to carry the child full-term. I would raise the child or place the child for adoption.

I was scared. I was alone.

I knew I could do better.

Interestingly, one of the things we had in common was a love for playing with kids.

Later, he said, "I love being like a kid. I don't want to have a kid."

Being Pregnant and Alone

Yes, being pregnant, young, and alone is very scary, but you get plenty of time to think about the kind of parent you want to be.

I started being more of a grownup, and he left me to find a more fun, and less complicated, girlfriend.

I got sober, went to therapy, found a better job, started to save, and removed myself from toxic people.

I started praying and listening to God more--about His thoughts of who I am and how He saw me.

I thought so little of myself that then I had both a mental and written list of what was wrong with me, and what I was lacking.

Today, I have learned to like and even love myself. Even all my messy parts.

I may not be everyone's cup of tea, but it is so freeing *when you learn to love yourself*.

I began listening to uplifting music. I stopped watching the news or anything negative. I started taking steps in positive directions and thinking about the steps I was taking in my life--the thoughts I was thinking, what I was watching and listening to, and who I was spending time with.

Living Intentionally

I started living intentionally!

Some might call that living on purpose. Rather than simply reacting, I chose to live a planned and premeditated life.

Trust me, it was not one step forward and then straight ahead to a smooth life.

It was one step forward and two or three steps back on many days. I feel like it took me until I was 23, with weekly therapy, to finally feel the rhythm of starting to become who I was meant to be.

Deb, my amazing therapist, was gentle, kind, encouraging, and allowed me to feel all the feelings of my life to that point--including being so scared, and feeling alone as a young pregnant woman.

I had my son at 20, so not quite a teen mom. I felt young and afraid-- but I had created a strong support system. I felt ready to raise my son, and I had decided to raise him as a single mom and give him all the love and support that we all long for from our parents.

By then, I was beyond just surviving. I was not quite thriving, but I loved being a mom. I had a good job and I had more stability in my life.

Stability and security can be scary when you are not used to it. Chaos can feel more comfortable. Change is hard and sometimes, when you are used to the unhealthy, you can be drawn back into it.

By the time I was 25, I had bought my first home, had full time work, had finally earned my driver's license (at age 22), and had bought a car. *Life was looking up.*

Time had passed, and I was beginning to rise, just like banana bread in the oven.

Encouraging Others

I wrote this book to offer you grace and encouragement on your journey.

It is not a straight line.

It is not easy.

It takes many ingredients and tools to turn your life around and it takes time.

When we have patience and grace for ourselves in the process of change, it is a lot less painful to make the necessary changes.

Helping Others Make Changes

As a gym owner for 12 years, I helped thousands of clients make changes. Often, the internal changes were even more profound than the exterior. I saw their JOY, the energy, the hope, and happiness that comes from getting healthy.

Many of us need to make big changes in our life, from a place of being bruised emotionally, from instability, unhealthy relationships, dysfunction, unhealthy body, unhealthy finances, unhealthy career and unhealthy emotions.

It will take work, hard work. But it is so worth it when you do the work *and you can start to live free!*

This idea started me thinking, "I love banana bread and my life is a bit like taking a bruised banana and turning it into a sweet, warm loaf of banana bread."

The Recipe

Essential Ingredients:

- Bruised bananas
- Flour
- Salt
- Sugar
- Eggs
- Baking soda
- Vanilla

Optional:

- Chocolate chips
- Nuts

What We Put Into Life

We must start with three bruised bananas to create a base, giving a moist sweetness to absorb all the solid pieces we mix in.

Just like life, sometimes we are the bruised bananas.

We are the base for this recipe when we decide to do the work and make the changes needed in our lives.

Flour, for me, represents therapy or counseling.

This helped me to understand that I did not cause the pain of my childhood, and I did not deserve the challenges I had to face.

Support for the journey. I do not have to walk alone.

Salt is the many tears I cried that helped me heal and flush out the pain I had experienced.

Today, I am grateful that most of my tears come from laughing hard.

Tears are healing, hopeful, and part of the letting-go process.

No need to apologize.

When we cry, our tears allow emotion to leave our body. A much better choice than holding it inside our chest.

Sugar represents the sweet and uplifting music I listen to. No more exposure to the negative or scary for my ears.

I avoid the news, scary movies, harsh words, anything that triggers me, or brings back harsh moments of my upbringing.

Sugar is sweet like uplifting, positive music or romantic comedies.

I love everything to have a happy ending. I know that is not realistic, and it bothers some people that I feel this way--but I know firsthand how harsh life can be. I will do everything I can to protect the happiness I have found and worked hard to discover in my adult life.

Eggs represent healthy people and healthy boundaries related to unhealthy people. Eggs hold the recipe together--and boundaries sometimes hold me together.

Having boundaries has set me free from feeling guilty when I need to take a break from someone--when I need to limit time with them.

Having boundaries with unhealthy people allows you to still have these people in your life, but with clearly set limits.

Baking soda helps me rise. It represents my faith. It is me believing God has better plans for my life than I have for myself.

It reminds me to look up when I feel out of control and to remember that I am not in charge.

It brings me peace.

I love the Serenity prayer, so simple and yet so powerful.

Sometimes I will repeat it up to 50 times a day.

"God Grant me the SERENITY to accept the things I cannot change,
the COURAGE to change the things I can,
and the WISDOM to know the difference."

Vanilla is needed to mix up the flavors just like I need movement in my life every day.

I say, and believe, that movement is my medicine.

I go for walks multiple times a day. Slow walks. Dog walks. Fast walks. Friend walks.

Walks ground me, bring me back to the present, remind me where I am and what I can control, and what I should let go of.

I am blessed to now live by the beach, where I get to listen to the ocean while I walk daily, which calms my soul and brings me JOY all at the same time.

Just like vanilla, the ocean air is sweet and savory all in the same smell.

Vanilla, to me, is movement and the richness life has to offer.

Vanilla needs to be mixed in and swirled about. It changes color, like the ocean.

Movement and unpredictability, like the ocean and life.

Optional Ingredients in Life

Chocolate chips remind me to savor the sweetness of life.

I have given away hundreds of loaves of bread in my life to neighbors, friends, co-workers, and family. I believe everything in life is sweeter when we share it.

Giving the gift of food is a true joy to me because it reminds me that I no longer live in food scarcity, and instead I have more than enough to share. I believe gratitude is a good life--but a generous life is a great life!

Nuts add protein for strength, and are a great source of several nutrients. They also contain antioxidants to help relieve stress.

I feel like the recipe for banana bread represents finding the right career or calling. In my life, knowing that all the pain and challenges I went through serve a special purpose today, as I write and speak to encourage others on their journey.

Time, Heat and Waiting

We also need time and heat to rise to who we are meant to be, just as we need that time in the oven to make banana bread.

For me, that time is waiting while I do the work for life to be different, feel different, and look different.

I did all the work on myself while I waited.

Time and *heat*.

Formula for Life

No matter what we walk through in life, we can take lessons that we learn along the way and use them to encourage others to stay hopeful.

Our work can offer purpose and meaning to our lives.

I created a formula I like to teach others. If we are open and willing, we can take the pain of our past, mix it with the passion and energy that shows up in our body, and turn it into our purpose.

Pain + Passion = Purpose

In a Ziggy cartoon, Ziggy was looking up and saying, "Why me God?" And God looks back and says, "Why not?"

For me, the pain of my childhood gave me the drive to become the parent I never had.

Today, my purpose is to be a nurturer to anyone, of any age, that I meet who needs some encouragement on their journey.

Though I do not love any of the pain and challenges I have gone through, they help me be more compassionate and empathetic.

Once we have healed, we can use our struggle to serve others.

Living My Dream... What's Yours?

I have always been a summer lover and, recently, I finally got to live out my 30-year dream to move to the beach in Southwest Florida.

Sunshine and warm air lift my spirits everyday.

Like all good things though, I had to wait, save, and plan for this moment to be a reality.

Walking on the beach grounds me and lifts my spirit so I can show up as the person I want to be in the world.

I had to wait, save, and plan for this moment to be a reality.

Today, I can sit in my living room and watch the ocean waves. I can cross the street and walk the beach morning, noon, and night.

That might not be your dream, but ask yourself:
- What is your dream?
- What do you need to work on?
- What are your ingredients?
- What is your timeline?

Growing up in dysfunction, walking through pain, and leaving unhealthy relationships all take time.

Be gentle with yourself.

Don't judge yourself.

Don't let anyone tell you that you should be "over it" by now or that you are doing it wrong. Take your own time to be to where you are meant to be.

I am a work in progress and know it will take the rest of my life to get to where I want to be. I am willing to keep doing the work and reflection.

One interesting fact about banana bread is that the more bruised the bananas, the sweeter the flavor.

I think, the more we have been through, sometimes the kinder and more compassionate we come out the other side.

I believe in you!

Keep moving forward.

The world needs you.

Banana Bread Recipe

- 3 bruised bananas
- ¾ cup of sugar
- 1 tsp. baking soda
- 1½ cups of flour
- 2 eggs
- ½ tsp. salt
- 1 tbsp. vanilla

Optional:
- Chocolate chips
- Nuts

Bake at 350 for one hour--longer if it needs it. Poke it with a toothpick to see if it's done.

Then, enjoy!

As you savor the flavor, remember--just a couple of hours ago, this was just a bunch of bruised bananas.

My hope is that all that has bruised you in life will help to make you into a beautiful banana bread.

- ✓ We always have a choice whether to stay bruised and bitter or take our broken parts and turn them into warm, beautiful, sweet banana bread.
- ✓ Set a time line for your goals. Be accountable to yourself, and gentle with yourself as you heal and grow.
- ✓ Is today the day you start healing *your* bruises?

Other Books by Annie Meehan

Be the Exception: Your 7 Steps to Transformation

Paths, Detours & Possibilities

Be The Exception Gratitude Journal

Be The Exception Bible Study Companion Guide

Life Lessons from Fruit Series

The Pineapple Principle

Bruised to Beautiful,
Life Lessons from Bananas

Coming Soon – More in the *Life Lessons from Fruit* Series!

56

SPEAKER - AUTHOR - CONSULTANT

Annie Meehan is an enthusiastic keynote speaker and author who inspires, enlightens, and energizes her audiences with a clear message that spurs listeners to break counterproductive patterns and **Be the Exception!**

As a keynote speaker, she has presented to numerous corporations, associations, and non-profit organizations, providing actionable strategies to strategically manage change, recognize the enormous power of words, and eliminate excuses that keep people from attaining their goals.

Her passion and charisma engage

people in new and exciting ways, which inspires people to seize a more enriching and fulfilled path forward.

An expert on living an exceptional life, Annie has authored five additional motivational books. She has three adult children and lives in Fort Myers Beach, Florida with her husband, Greg. She loves volunteering in her community, traveling with her family, and walking (or being walked) with her two dogs, Peanut and Leo!

To learn more about Annie and her work, contact here at:

www.AnnieMeehan.com

Annie@AnnieMeehan.com

952-994-8356

Speaking Testimonials

"The greatest gift I gave to the audience at our recent conference was having Annie as the opening keynote. She imbued such an incredibly positive and hopeful vibe among the attendees that it lasted the entire 2 day event. Annie is a class-act, a sparkplug, a ball of energy, and a love letter all wrapped up in a tiny package..."

Joe Webb
President,
DealerKnows

"... Annie brings hope to her audience through practical skills, storytelling, and personal awareness. She becomes part of the audience, and not just while on stage, but forever. Unlike many speakers you can hire to "deliver" a "speech", Annie engulfs herself with your group and bonds with people. She creates relationships and continues to mentor, educate and inspire for days, weeks and months after her stage performance is over..."

Pamela Shepherd
The Global Event Team

"Annie Meehan recently to spoke to a an event focused on women for our firm. She was outstanding - one of the best speakers I have ever seen. She made us laugh, made us cry and more importantly made us think. A great message of telling ourselves the right story and taking care of ourselves and others. I would highly recommend Annie to speak at any group."

Ryan J Kramer
Managing Partner
Northwestern Mutual
Chicagoland

"Annie is a phenomenal speaker. Her presence is so positive, friendly and approachable. She was the keynote at our tech company's first annual client event and she was a perfect fit. I highly recommend Annie for any kind of speaking engagement or conference. We can't wait to work with our new friend Annie again!"

Angie Heck
IT Project Manger

Image Attributions

Images courtesy of
OpenClipart.org.

All images licensed under the
Creative Commons Zero 1.0 Public
Domain License

Cover art by Iaria.

Made in the USA
Middletown, DE
26 October 2022

13511190R00040